MURPHY'S LAW

Commandments and corollaries of
Murphy's Original Law of Inevitable Disaster.
Dedicated to the dismalness of human nature and
the certainty of cruel fate.

MURPHY'S
LAW

Jim Russell

Art by
Russ Youngreen

CELESTIAL ARTS
Millbrae, California

First Printing, February 1978
Made in the United States of America

Library of Congress Cataloging in Publication Data

Russell, Jim, 1931-
    Russell on Murphy's law.

    1. Murphy's law.   I.   Title.
PN6231.M82R87   818'.5'407   77-90023
ISBN 0-89087-224-4

        3   4   5   6   7   —   84   83   82   81   80   79   78

Contents

Acknowledgments

My thanks to a couple of malcontents named Lee James and Tom Parry who, along with many others, contributed reams of theoretical pie. The various derivations of the Law of Duality first appeared in *Northliner* Magazine in an article entitled "Beyond Murphy's Law" by Walter Mulé. Finally my special appreciation to John D. Hutchens and Mary Ness for persisting in the idea that Murphy belonged to the world.

Messrs. Al Uhl and Gerald Norbury, editors of the *Honeywell World,* who are perhaps looking here for an acknowledgment of their helpful guidance, may continue to look.

The Law of the Jungle

I think most of us have a positive outlook on life. We muck along, expecting things to turn out well. It's part of that thing called the Puritan Ethic we're supposed to have inherited. Work hard and you will succeed. Dream the impossible dream. Every frog an unkissed prince.

It has been said that to write truly beautiful music, first you must hear the angels sing. And oh, how we listen. Our basic mind-set is that if anything can go right, it will. Right? I mean, hardly anyone tells us to try for a pie in the face, a nail in the tire or a clinker on the clarinet. These are not proper goals at all.

Dare to be great, they tell us. And so we stroll down life's highway, eyes to the sky, oblivious to the chuckholes underfoot—and there are chuckholes. Mother Nature is remarkably evenhanded in dishing up the lumps with the gravy.

The Trouble with Statisticians

Statisticians have determined that there is absolutely no outcome that has a mathematical probability of zero. Almost zero maybe, but not quite. Anything and everything has some remote possibility of coming to pass. At any given moment, they will tell you, it is highly unlikely that the molecules of wood in the chair you are sitting on will suddenly rearrange themselves in such a way as to cause the chair to collapse and hurl you to the floor. But, there is some slight probability greater than zero that it might happen.*

Might happen, nonsense! It will happen, and at any moment! That chair is just waiting for you to relax and let your guard down for an instant so it can break your silly neck. Why? Because there is a law on the books called *Murphy's Law* that suspends the law of probability and, from time to time, most of the other ones as well. If a thing has some remote possibility of going wrong, says Murphy, it will go wrong. Those statisticians are no better than the Puritans. Instead of telling us to put our trust in wooden chairs and sleeping rattlesnakes and the Dow-Jones Average, they should be telling us to up our major medical. Where the numbers boys got off the track, it seems to me, is in the misapplication of their own probability theories. While there are only a few ways of doing a thing right, there are infinite ways of doing them wrong. It's as simple as that.

---

*The flip side of this proposition is that nothing has a 100% probability of happening either. I read with interest in a science mag that astrophysicists have determined that light never quite achieves the speed of light.

Monkey Business Understood

Are things really that bad? One is left to ponder how, if things are foreordained to screw up, we have managed to survive as well as we have. Prosper even. Given the stern dicta of natural selection (natural rejection, really), how did homo sapiens, that frail clod with no pelt and an overbite, ever manage to make it down out of his tree and survive a hostile environment that is obviously out to get him?

Certainly not by taking life too seriously, for reality is a bad trip. The fact is, mankind has a secret weapon, more powerful than Mother Nature's most malevolent molecule: the clod has a sense of humor. It's probably all that saves us. By laughing at the odds, we hang onto our sanity and keep on trudging after the grail.

Thoughts on Tragedy

Anything that can go wrong, will go wrong. If it wasn't funny, it would be tragic. But isn't all humor essentially tragic? The hotfoot. Mud on the petticoat. The snowball's fatal attraction for the silk hat. These all speak of suffering and frustration, yet we guffaw. And by finding release in the other fellow's misfortunes we learn to endure our own. And therein lies our salvation.

Anything that can go wrong, will go wrong. The very statement has the ring of the ages. It is Everyman's suit of armor for the flung pies of life.

We give the statement a name. We call it Murphy's Law, which somehow makes it even funnier, and we apply it with the precision of a Gladstone to the tribulations that beset us at home and at work. Murphy's Law may well be the most powerful tool we possess for survival in this civilized jungle we inhabit. It certainly is our wackiest.

Enter Murphy, Laughing

Speaking of laws, they run our lives to a larger extent than most of us care to admit. For cautious people who appreciate a well-ordered existence, this comes as comforting news. But even the freest spirit among us wears shackles from which there is, alas, no escape.

Some laws, engineered into the very cosmos, dog us every minute of the day. Gravity. Inertia. Weather. They dictate everything from the height one can leap at a single bound to the weight a wet garbage sack can support before giving way. You can't beat these laws. Early on, you learn to cope.

Other laws, man-made, are a bit more qualitative, but you usually know when and where they lurk and can chart your course accordingly. Traffic regulations. Property rights. Incestual taboos. They decree, for example, that you must honk your horn if you love Jesus or hate that idiot ahead of you who is turning left in midblock, but must shush when entering hospital zones and public libraries. For most people, life's a lot easier when treading these paths of righteousness with reasonable care.

About Ointment and the Fly

Easier, that is, except sometimes. For that one little fly in the ointment, Murphy's Law, not only upsets the apple cart, it topples the whole blooming orchard. It zonks us at the darnedest times and in the darnedest ways. It is the certain harbinger of the unbidden pie in the face, the nail in the tire and the clinker on the clarinet. It gives new meaning to the concept of retribution for Original Sin.

Murphy's Law governs a world where the toast always falls jelly-side down and firecrackers sputter harmlessly until picked up. It is a world peopled with the long-suffering likes of Joe Btfsplk and Ziggy, the ever-hovering black cloud and the resigned rainee. It is the world in which you and I must spend the rest of our lives.

The Roger Pembrook Syndrome

Last spring, a few days after Easter, it warmed up in Quincy, Massachusetts. Roger Pembrook wandered into his garage, filled with that once-a-year urge to "do something to the yard." He was clearly not himself or he might have recognized the danger signals. Selecting his ammunition from a dimly lit assortment of barbecue, automotive, and landscaping paraphernalia, Roger set to work, humming.

In no time at all he managed to spread Vita-Gro on the dandelions, dust Weed-B-Dead on his tomato plants and, exhausted, plop himself into a resurrected hammock with a beer. Peace and self-righteousness fell lightly on his beaming countenance. Thy job be done.

Later, as the tomato plants shriveled to black ribbons and the dandelion crop shot up waist-high, reality crept into Roger's noggin: Somewhere in his brief burst of horticultural zeal, something had gone wrong. With the best of motives, he had committed a klutzy blunder. Or had he?

Oh, at first he did suffer pangs of self-reproach. But the more he thought about it, the more the truth came clear—Roger Pembrook of Quincy, Massachusetts, had been visited by that most dread of all natural forces: Murphy's Law.

It mattered little that the garage was so dark that he couldn't read the labels. It was equally unimportant that the weeds would probably have prospered and the tomatoes eventually withered even if Roger had decided to play golf instead of God that day. The simple fact is that the original remote possibility of his getting the poison mixed up with the fertilizer had turned into a virtual certainty by the perverse machinations of that nasty law.

In this case it was bad news for the tomatoes, good news for the dandelions and fantastic news for Roger, who sighed the sigh of one who is suddenly off the hook. How could it be his fault? It was just another case of Murphy's Law.

The Case for Bracing

The proposition Murphy poses is a simple one: *In any field of human endeavor, anything that can possibly go wrong, will go wrong, and at the worst possible time.*

What's so complicated about that? The law has not come to light so newly that its precise formulation may be considered more than a refinement.

Murphy's Law has been recognized and dreaded for centuries. Today, millions of people in every corner of the planet brace themselves daily, wary of its sudden, devastating effects. Can you do less?

How It
All Begun,
Sort Of

As indicated previously, the human animal ran into trouble early in the game. Lions kept getting into the caves. The wheel would not hold air. Primitive war clubs splintered when struck on the trademark. Clearly, something was coming between man and his aspirations. But what? Archaeologists have painstakingly pieced together early attempts to explain the Murphy phenomenon.

When the Great Pyramid was opened and the burial chamber unsealed for the first time in 4,000 years, it was found to be empty. No mummy, no nothing. With 30 years of hard labor and several thousand tons of chiseled rock into the project, the Egyptian royal family obviously meant to bury somebody in there, somebody pretty darned important from the looks of things. But something went wrong and they sealed 'er up empty. Evidence that the ancient Egyptians understood what they were

up against has been found in one of the tomb's hieroglyphic inscriptions: "The winds of the desert blow in inverse ratio to the need for sand." The author of this ageless wisdom is thought to be none other than Merf-a-mem-non, the tutor of Tut.

The glory that was Greece came a cropper when the Greek navy, the pride of Athens and the terror of the Aegean, sailed off to conquer tiny, far-off Sicily. Although the attacking fleet consisted of the mightiest of fighting ships and carried legions of well-equipped soldiers, the spunky islanders whipped them soundly. This didn't sit too well with the taxpayers back home and things went from bad to worse for the Greek military-industrial complex from then on. A tattered piece of sailcloth, found among the remnants of that once-mighty armada, bears witness to the agony of military defeat. Scrawled on this musty fabric are the words: "As ye sew, so shall ye rip." It is signed by Morphopolous, tailor to his majesties, Euripides and Eumenides.

Much has been written of the decline and fall of the Roman Empire, but where did it all begin? What little thing went wrong? One is left to ponder a line of graffiti carved on the wall of an ancient pizzeria: "The pasta is always tougher than the stamina of the chewer." Since Caesar's army traveled on its stomach, the author of this gem had clearly stumbled onto something basic. Confucius could not have said it better.

And, speaking of the Venerable One, China still boasts of its Great Wall, standing after twenty-three centuries, solemn testimony to the military foresight of the Chinese emperor, Chin, who built it.

Fifty feet high, 25 feet thick and 1,200 miles long, the wall gave China absolute protection from its marauding Mongol neighbors. The Mongolian hordes, who didn't realize this, merely walked around the end and mopped up on the snoozing Chinese. It was not Confucius but the vanquished general Mor-fu, who shook his head ruefully and moaned: "If only we had built the wall just a little bit longer!"

It is clear from the foregoing that disaster, unexpected and unpreventable, is an essential part of the human equation. The gradual derivation of Murphy's Law over agonizing centuries attests to its basic and enduring qualities. Yet for all the wisdom of the ages, we are no less vulnerable today. It can flatten angel food cakes as easily as it toppled dynasties. Like the ancients, we can define the law and study it *ad infinitum*, but alas, we can no more repeal it than we can repeal the law of gravity.

And speaking of gravity, history records that when Herb Newton was struck on the head while sitting under a fig tree, he put cause and effect together in a law which he stated as: "Unplucked figs plunk." This became known as Fig Newton's Law, but it never caught on in the textbooks.

That's Murphy's Law for you!

Variations on a Theme by Catastrophius

Murphy's Law has heretofore been presented as a single, simple statement: *Anything that can go wrong, will go wrong.* This is by no means the only version of the law. Look at the bulletin board in any office or factory and you'll see Murphy's offspring in assorted sizes and shapes, each tailored to the work at hand and the local author's unhappy experience. Look under the magnetic daisies on any suburban refrigerator and you'll find that homebodies find solace in Murphy's weird workings, too.

Some otherwise sensible people actually dispute the finer points of the law, locking in hot debate over the authenticity of a given version. There are those who insist that anything other than the "can go wrong, will go wrong" commandment is pure heresy. Others fall in behind the more pragmatic "jelly-side down" fable. Many brandish faded

Xerox copies of their favorite law as documented
evidence. I wonder if Moses had this problem.

Pie Theory Explained

To end what is really an idle argument, everybody is
correct. Murphy knows no limitations in dealing out
life's lumps. There is a basic set of statements, however, which scholars believe embody the basic ele-
ments of the master's General Law.

In order to understand their derivation, it is
first necessary to learn a few technical terms asso-
ciated with what scientists have come to call Pie
Theory or Piemanship Dynamics.

Piemanship—The body of knowledge which deals with the dynamic and perverse behavior of inanimate objects in proximity to mortals.

Pie—A metaphoric missive. Solid, gelatinous or verbal. Unexpected by the recipient. Also unwanted.

Pieman—The recipient of the Murphian Meringue. Pure of heart and therefore ripe for pie. (Derivation is believed to be from the French: *le pigeon.*)

Pie Theory is still a very new field of study and the accumulated research documentation is not great. Most of the early work was done by Dr. Edsel Tucker of Catatonic State. It was he who first postulated such theorems as "Pie in the sky is sweet, by and by" and "Pie are square."* Besides the derivation of Murphy's six general expressions below, Dr. Tucker is perhaps best remembered for a statement contained in the syllabus for his *Ethics of Pastry C3* course: "Every man a pieman, every pie a hummer." I think you get the drift of it.

---

*Tucker's archrival, Professor Berry "Yum Yum" Tartman of Amagonagat U., successfully refuted this by demonstrating that pie are round. "Cornbread," he asserted, "are square."

General Expression #1

Anything that can go wrong, will go wrong.

This most fundamental statement of Murphy's Law is positional in nature. It may be described mathematically by a three-dimensional computer model which plots the strivings of the pieman, the trajectory of the pie, and the awkwardness of their conjuncture. All of the conditions of the model are met when pie and pieman arrive at intersecting cross hairs simultaneously. Data processing experts find it awesome that Mother Nature pulls this off thousands of times a day using only a slide rule.

General Expression #2

Things will go wrong at the worst
possible time.

This adds Einstein's fourth dimension, time, to the
other three. A more complex computer model is
therefore required to simulate pieman's hour-by-
hour anxieties and expectations, calculating the
single most embarrassing or damaging moment for
pie arrival. The programmer at his option may adjust either pieman's location, the trajectory of the
oncoming pie or the position of the cross hairs for
maximum effect. It would never do to have the cat
bring in the dead mouse *before* the tea guests arrive.
Or after they leave.

General Expression #3

> If there is a possibility of several things going wrong, the one that will go wrong is the one that will do the most damage.

Value judgments are very important here, so the computer model must be constructed so as to solve two or more differential equations at once, based on the relative consequences that can be expected from various kinds of pies—*as assessed by pieman himself.* To satisfy the model, pieman and the right flavored pie must hit the cross hairs at the worst possible moment. This becomes easier as the programmer becomes familiar with pieman's frailties. Mother Nature, of course, already knows them. (Note: For this and subsequent simulations, it is recommended that the computer be coated with Teflon for ease of cleaning.)

General Expression #4

> Left to themselves, things will go from bad to worse.

Remarkable as it may seem, this statement of the law is equally valid if the first part is reversed to read:

> When properly attended to, things will go from bad to worse.

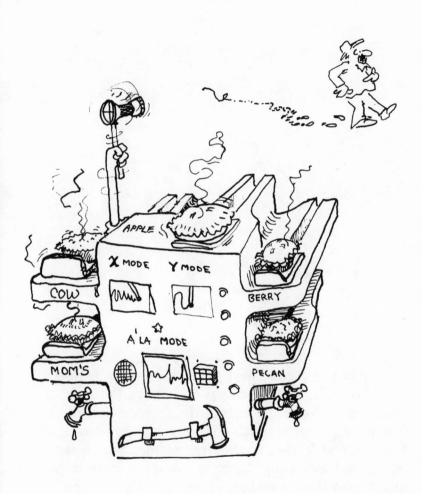

Yes, only the second part of the statement is opera-
tive. To believe otherwise is to believe that pieper-
sons can mitigate their fate. In this version of the
law we are dealing with the very tricky concept of
latency, also known as the ripple effect, which so far
has defied modeling. Your average pie, once wiped
away, has little residual clout. Your truly cosmic
pie, however, wounds and wounds again. After taking an incoming Waterloo Meringue, Napoleon Bo-
naparte wallowed in pie for the rest of his life.

General Expression #5

> Nature always sides with the hidden
> flaw.

Here we have a ball bearing assembly containing 16 small, perfectly spherical steel balls, burnished to mirror brightness and tempered in simmering peanut oil. This marvel of frictionless rotation is designed to operate for 10,000 hours minimum without so much as a drop of oil. Now introduce a single microscopic piece of grit. Nature will completely ignore the engineering genius and costly processes that went into the burnishing and tempering of those glorious little balls and throw in its lot with the grit. Result: the bearing burns out in 45 minutes, taking a 50-horsepower dynamo with it. This seems grossly unfair until you stop to realize that a very basic characteristic of Murphy's Law is that it is grossly unfair. Always remember, Nature never sides with pieman.

General Expression #6

> If everything seems to be going well,
> you have obviously overlooked some-
> thing.

Don't take the "you" in this expression personally.
It *refers* to some hapless pieman, not an intelligent
and informed person like yourself. Having read this
far, you have learned that complex mathematical relationships are in motion all around you. You know
that your innermost hopes and worries are an open
book to the master programmer with the Irish
brogue. You understand all too well that, even now,
dreadful pies are being aimed and cocked with
frightening accuracy. The concept of "going well"
has been erased from your consciousness; you are
forearmed and ever wary. (WHOOPS! I do believe
your chair has collapsed, hurling you to the floor.
That *is* a nasty welt on your neck!)

So far we have dealt only with the probability of undesirable things happening to the undesirer. That probability, we have learned, is right around 100%. But there is an equally dismal alternative on the other face of the coin—that hoped-for events will *not* transpire.

The Heartbreak of Murphy's Reverse Law

Pieman sits in the cloakroom, nervously awaiting the election results that will name him Grand Horn Bearer of the Loyal Order of Rams. In the confusion, a majority of the ballots cast for good old pieman by his many friends and business associates are mistakenly tallied for a brother Ram who stammers badly and dreads the prospect of horndom. Pieman, of course, loses by one vote and, along with the newly elected G-g-g-great Horn B-b-b-bearer, takes to drink. A double whammy!

In dealing with the non-happening of expected events, our mathematical task is much simpler. There are no unknowns, no trajectories to trace, no cross hairs to adjust. There is only a large, inevitable zero to crank into the equation, which as any eighth-grader will tell you, renders all other parts of the equation equal to zero. Or to put it even more simply:

$$1 + 1 \quad \text{☞} \quad 2$$

where ☞ is a symbol meaning *hardly ever.*

Murphy's Law of Duality Examined

The basic law works beautifully in predicting the character of individual outcomes. It explains why, for example, a $300 color TV picture tube will protect a 10¢ fuse by blowing first. It falls short of perfection, however, where two outcomes are possible. For this we must turn to a refinement of General Expression #3 *(If there is a possibility of several things going wrong, the one that will go wrong is the one that will do the most damage),* called the Law of Duality. Consider the Putnam Phenomenon.

On November 30, 1972, Fred Putnam invited his girl friend over for an evening in front of a cozy fire. He used two boxes of matches, one pint of starter fluid, the Sunday edition of the New York Times and failed utterly to get a single flicker of flame started. Bent on romance by firelight at any

cost, he drove with his girl friend to the Hideaway Lodge, a fireplace-equipped hostelry in the nearby mountains. On the way, he lit a cigarette, threw the match out the car window and started a forest fire that devastated 382 acres of timber and burned the Hideaway Lodge to cinders.

Poking through the ashes, insurance investigator I. Burnham stumbled upon the Axiom of Probable Misfortune, to wit: *Of two possible events, only the undesired one will occur.* (Unfortunately, this is Mr. Burnham's only contribution to Pie Theory. His promising career was cut short by a skydiving accident where he had to choose between a parachute and a seat cushion.) This was not the end of research on dual events, however, as witness the Winkles-Greenspiel Manifestation.

On October 3, 1975, Irving Winkles, using a portable computer and a program he had taken six years to work out, lost every penny of his savings in a Las Vegas keno game. The same day, in the casino next door, Mrs. Emmajean Greenspiel, a 72-year-old widow, picked a 12-spot winner that netted her $17,500 the first and only time she ever played keno. She had bet the ages of her grandchildren.

Tucker, Tartman and others saw in this a more precise working of duality than theorized by Burnham, and the Theorem of Perverse Duality gradually evolved. Actual authorship of the law, which states that *the probability of a given event occurring is inversely proportional to its desirability,* is still hotly contested. (Tucker has the overwhelming body of evidence in his favor, lending credence to those who believe it should properly be called Tartman's Law.)

We may mathematically express the Theorem of Perverse Duality this way:

$$P = \frac{1}{D}$$

where P is probability and D is desirability. As one goes up, the other goes down in a most perverse manner. Again, the classical statisticians had been proved wrong by Murphian mathematics. While they would have you believe that the probability of an event happening would be distributed along a normal curve something like this,

P

the introduction of a desirability vector skews the curve sharply to the left, like this:

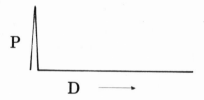

When it was announced in *Pie Quarterly*, the Theorem of Perverse Duality had immediate practical value in the field. At last, pie theorists had something of substance with which to explain why, for example, the person holding the most raffle tickets has the least chance of winning. There now remains one last fillip to be added before we can arrive at a true General Law of Duality. Desperate times are said to breed great leaders and at this precise moment in the evolution of duality theory, an acknowledged genius in Pie Dynamics strode forth with the missing puzzle piece: The concept of *effort*. Thus we have:

$$ P = \frac{1}{E \times D} $$

where P is probability, D is desirability and E is effort. The General Law of Duality, then, reads: *The probability of a given event occurring is inversely proportional to its desirability multiplied by the effort expended to achieve it.* Voila! Amazingly accurate, astonishingly simple! (Modesty prevents me from revealing the name of the crack mathematician responsible for this breakthrough.)

Obviously, the harder you try, the less likely you are to succeed, because as the denominator gets larger through increased effort, the value of P gets smaller. That is why Putnam could not get his fireplace started and why Winkles couldn't possibly hope to win at keno.

Conversely, as the value of E diminishes, the greater the probability of the event coming to pass.

For this reason, the Hideaway Lodge is rubble and Emmajean Greenspiel is dripping rhinestones. One need not go far afield with this line of reasoning to perceive how an indolent electorate provides fertile ground for mischief in government. It is sound Pie Theory and superlative Murphy.

Which reminds me of another of Edsel Tucker's rallying cries. "Pie," he would remark, slapping his gut, "is just desserts!"

The People's Choice

Murphy's Law truly belongs to the people. Classic expressions of the law were all gleaned from the bulletin boards of business and industry. Although less well-known than the General Expressions, they address a broad spectrum of Murphian mischief and provide new perspectives on Pie Theory.

A later chapter, Occupational Hazards, deals with specific instances of on-the-job obfuscation, but these pronouncements speak with a near-universal tongue of man's eternal frustration. Remember that series of inspirational readings published under the heading "Words to Live By"? These, friends, are words to perish by!

Nothing is as easy as it looks.

Think about this the next time you raise the hood of your car to check out the latest funny sound. Seems to be coming from inside the carburetor, doesn't it? Faced with this seemingly simple troubleshooting exercise, your average pieman will never ask himself these two all-important little questions: "Do I know anything at all about carburetors?" and "Can I learn to live with that funny sound?" Or, if he asks them, he fails to answer them no-yes. That's what makes him a pieman.

If you fool around with a thing for very long you will screw it up.

Well, here you are, laying the parts of your carburetor out on the fender of your car, protecting the rusted finish with a *"hers"* hand towel. Some of the pieces that resisted removal appear somewhat bent. Three things are becoming obvious: 1) You have no idea which doo-jiggy might have caused the noise. 2) You have no idea what order things go back in. 3) Nothing seems to fit any more. Gee, that noise was hardly noticeable at all.

> Once something is screwed up,
> anything done to improve it will make
> it worse.

A little twist with the pliers here, a tap with the mallet there, a dab of Elmer's on the torn gasket, and finally everything is tucked safely back under the hood (except one spring which doesn't seem to belong anywhere). At start-up, your engine gives one earsplitting roar that subsides only when the ignition is turned off. Then, nothing. You have the puddle of gasoline under the car mopped up in no time.

> Fixing a thing takes longer and costs
> more than you thought.

You ride up front with the tow truck driver on the way over to Charlie's Exxon. The pimply kid by the grease rack, the one who did so miserably as your paperboy a few years back, fills out an ominous repair sheet and tells you to call back tomorrow. (Is he hiding a smirk?) It later develops that a rebuilt carburetor for your model is not available in town and for three days you make the 30-mile trip to the plant and back by taxi.

> It is easier to get into something than
> to get out of it.

At last, the engine hums like a top. But that funny noise is louder than ever. You think maybe it's coming from the clutch . . . .

> **If you try to please everybody, nobody will like it.**

I thought surely this expression had been contributed by a politician, perhaps a congressman on one of the agricultural committees. Checking my files, I discovered that it came out of middle management at American Motors, the folks who surveyed public tastes and came out in 1976 with the AMC Pacer. (The guy swears the quotation originated with the 1946 Studebaker, but that's probably just a case of autosuggestion.)

> **If you need a thing, you will have thrown it away.**
> *Alternate:* **If you throw a thing away, you will need it.**

Determining cause and effect can get a little tricky. Does the absence of a thing create its necessity or is it the other way around? For want of a nail, the shoe was lost, but would keeping an extra nail on hand guarantee that anyone would want it or the shoe? Or, would it perhaps guarantee that nobody would want either one? I suspect the latter and therefore prefer a somewhat different construction of the law, to wit:

> **If you keep a thing in case you need it, you will not need it.**

Whatever you want to do, you have to
do something else first.

Around the time America decided to put a man on
the moon, someone developed a scheduling disci-
pline called PERT, Program Evaluation with Re-
spect to Time. Every moon-related project was as-
signed a PERT man who analyzed the various tasks
on a time continuum and identified *critical paths*,
key steps that would create utter havoc with the
rest of the program if not accomplished in timely
fashion. The PERT man placed the highest priority
on protecting these critical paths from delay, as-
signing extra expediters, coordinators, and super-
visors. With so much extraneous manpower swarm-
ing around, responsibilities got fuzzy and eventually somebody fumbled the ball to the detriment of
the entire space program. Only after the critical
path concept was abandoned did it become feasible
to reach the moon in our time and take "one small
step." PERT still represents one of the finest flow-
erings of Murphy's Law.

No good deed goes unpunished.

If the road to hell is paved with good intentions, the
road to heaven may be paved with unrewarded acts
of piety. Even our old friends, the Puritans, thought
so. Did I say unrewarded? Faith and bejabbers,
Murphy rewards every act of piety with (what else?)
pie. It is not by chance that little old ladies lash out
at helpful Boy Scouts. It is the way of the world.

Nature is a mother.

This underscores the paranoia engendered by the
understanding and acceptance of Murphy's Law.
Even as we try our hardest to persevere, every
stepping-stone turns to cowflop as we press our
weight upon it. The very forces of nature seem ar-
rayed against us. Admission of paranoia is general-
ly thought to be the beginning of recovery. In this
case, however, recovery is fatal. Someone *is* out to
get us. Think about this the next time you see a
truck labeled *Ma's Pies.*

Don't mess with Mrs. Murphy!

You figure that one out.

Occupational Hazards

The invisible legislature that keeps passing new amendments to Murphy's Law is most active in the offices and factories of the nation. Here, there is ready access to (1) glaring examples of the law at work and (2) copying machines. The result is an outpouring of pungent humor that holds a warped fun house mirror to the idiosyncrasies of the particular industry or occupation.

Since it only takes one vote to amend Murphy's Law, and since the delegates are in session three shifts a day, there is no way to capture more than a glimpse of the total picture. It's enough, though, to prove that the law touches God's creatures in all walks of life with evenhanded irreverence and that boredom on the job yields to Murphy more often than Muzak.

To the lawgivers in every field of endeavor, I offer the time-honored Latin toast: *Bastardus non carborundum.* Don't let the front office grind you down.

On the Line and In the Shop

Mechanical things seem especially prone to Murphy's Law. The more precisely they are engineered, the more gloriously they malfunction. The more useful the work they perform, the more inconvenient their lapses. And despite the best efforts of factory hands and repairmen to keep them humming, the task is insurmountable. If Murphy was born in the Garden of Eden, he reached puberty at the dawn of the Industrial Revolution and today enjoys his nasty old manhood on the nearest production line. The resulting anarchy of inanimate objects begets more Murphyesque mathematica than all of the other professions combined. It is from this outpouring that the following have been culled:

Interchangeable parts won't.

Identical units tested under identical conditions will not behave identically after installation.

Dimensions will always be expressed in the least usable terms. Velocity, for example, will be expressed in furlongs per fortnight.

The availability of a part is inversely proportional to the need for that part.

A device selected at random from a lot having 99% reliability will belong to the 1% group.

Leakproof seals will.

Self-starters will not.

If a project requires "n" components, there will be "n-1" units in stock.

The firmness of a delivery date is inversely proportional to the tightness of the schedule.

A failure will not occur until after the device has passed Final Inspection.

Ideas adopted from the Suggestion Box will increase costs and reduce quality.

A fail-safe circuit will destroy those around it.

The relationship between the direction of motor rotation and the arrow on the cover is random.

The White Collar Zoo

In any business office, there is a tremendous amount of mental energy expended in trying to beat the system. No matter that the system is unbeatable. Everyone accepts that. There is apparently as much satisfaction to be derived from pelting management with an unending array of unflattering observations as there would be in actually toppling the *status quo.* It also helps that your average business executive, by his demeanor, practically begs for pie.

Murphy's Law is an apt vehicle for describing the sorry state of bossdom and the boss-dominated hierarchy. But, alas, it accounts not only for the muck at the top but the mire at the bottom as well. Myopia, thy name is Pieman. Nevertheless, that these expressions ignore the nether portions of the white-collar power pyramid is due less to oversight on the part of the water-cooler gang than to the illiteracy of those smug bastards at the top.

No job is too difficult for the individual with vision, stamina and the power to delegate.

When communications are improved between different levels in an organization, the result is a vastly increased area of misunderstanding.

The effort expended in defending an error is in direct proportion to the magnitude of the error.

The substitution of computers for people invariably leads to a net increase in staff.

Alternate: Increased automation of clerical functions invariably results in increased operational costs.

When it is not necessary to make a decision, it is neccesary not to make a decision. (Not necessarily.)

When exaggerated emphasis is placed on delegation, responsibility, like sediment, sinks to the bottom.

The legibility of shorthand notes is inversely proportional to the importance of the dictation.

Garbage in, garbage out. (Bet you thought we forgot.)

The Political Arena

It's a small hop and jump from office politics to the other kind. Given the venal predilections of the untreed ape, it's easy to see why so few lawmakers escape Murphy's Law. It was Will Rogers who said, "This country has come to feel the same when Congress is in session as when the baby gets hold of a hammer." And even before Watergate, he cracked "I don't make up jokes. I just read the paper and report the news." The following punditry was contributed in equal measure by weary laymen and candid public servants. It's further proof, as if any

were needed, that Murphy is alive and well in every corner of bureaucratic officialdom from Congress to the county courthouse.

Where you stand on an issue depends on where you sit.

It is easier to be a liberal a long way from home.

Anything based on greed and avarice is on a firm footing and will prevail.

The light at the end of the tunnel is the headlamp of an oncoming train.

Any facts which do not support a position will be suppressed.

We have more to fear from the bungling of the incompetent than from the machinations of the wicked.

As the economy gets better, everything else gets worse.

The length of debate is inversely proportional to the complexity of the issue. (Thus, if the issue is simple enough, debate approaches infinity. See Parkinson's Law.)

"The more he spoke of his honor, the faster we counted our spoons." (Charles Dickens)

SKROINK

Do It (to) Yourself

Judging from the notes tacked up on the kitchen cupboards of America, the average husband is ⅓ cockeyed optimist, ⅓ Dagwood Bumstead and ⅓ bandaids. (We have already met that modern day Luther Burbank, Roger Pembrook, with his withered tomatoes and giant dandelions.) Wives fare much better, but that is probably because they are the only ones who know where the tacks are. Murphy in the home is Murphy rampant. He provides cradle-to-the-grave coverage on everything from school projects to home improvements, with special attention given to anything with an expired warranty. *Do it yourself* was the handyman's proud battlecry until the red-haired leprechaun turned it into a thumb-throbbing whimper. Read on, Mr. and Mrs. Homemaker. This page is yours.

All warranties expire upon payment of the invoice.

Any tool dropped while repairing an automobile will roll underneath to the exact center.

The repairman will never have seen a model quite like yours before.

Any wire, pipe, or board cut to exact length will be 5/8-inch too short.

When a misbehaving appliance is demonstrated for the repairman, the appliance will work like new.

After a major appliance has been repaired and reassembled, parts will be noticed on the floor.

The tool required to complete your repairs is on the other truck.

The other truck is in the shop.

The shop is closed today. Sorry.

Professional Wisdom

Certainly we can look to the halls of academia for
shelter from the mean, green marauder. Here, logic
and sanity prevail. Here, brave men quake at the
mere thought of a miscalculation, an error in judg-
ment or (ugh!) an accident. There is absolutely no
room for things going wrong in the professions.
Wrong! The smarter they are, the harder they fall.
We have already witnessed the embarrassment
Murphy visited on the statistical smarties who had
suggested that the probability of a screw-up could
be calculated on a normal curve. Well, the rest of the
mortarboard crew is mortal, too. Doctors bury their
mistakes, according to the old saw, but scientists
publish theirs. What? You're still in doubt? Just
peruse the following items.

> Academic arguments are the most vi-
> cious and bitter because (a) the
> stakes are so low and (b) the issues
> have been decided five years previ-
> ously. (Higher education)

> The darker your skin pigmentation,
> the nearer you sit to the front win-
> dow. (Industrial genetics)

> For every human act there are two
> reasons: the stated one and the real
> one. These have a correlation coeffi-
> cient very close to zero. (Behavioral
> sciences)

No amount of genius can overcome a preoccupation for detail. (Applied research)

To know thyself is the ultimate form of aggression. (Freudian psychology)

Under carefully controlled conditions, organisms under study will behave as they jolly well please. (Biochemistry)

Everything east of the San Andreas Fault will eventually plunge into the Atlantic Ocean. (Seismology)

Other
People's
Laws

In the quest for logic amongst the pratfalls, Murphy is not alone. Pie lore contains the names of other men who have stared in awe at the frailty of human nature and certainty of cruel fate. Parkinson and Peter leap to mind immediately, giants both, but there are others who have perceived dark relationships and written laws.* It is somewhat unfortunate that many of these formidable formulae live on in the names of their authors rather than of the Hibernian Hexer who begat them. Each of the latter-day scholars has studied, unwittingly perhaps, at the knee of the master. Make no mistake, Murphy's is not the most important law. It is the *only* law.

---

*For example, Gresham's Law (bad books drive out good books) is beautifully illustrated by the fact that you purchased this book.

The Parkinson Principle

Parkinson started out with a fairly simple putdown
on the bureaucrat lurking in us all:

> Work expands to fill the available
> time.

The world fell in love with it immediately. Although
simply stated, there's nothing small about the idea.
We've all been there and the proof pops up all the
time. Earlier, we encountered:

> The length of debate is inversely pro-
> portional to the complexity of the
> issue. (By golly, we encountered it
> again!)

Fellow procrastinators have penned:

> Time spent on any project will be in-
> versely proportional to its impor-
> tance. (An organization with very little
> available time will thus have an infi-
> nite capacity for trivia. I know. I usta
> work there.)

And again:

> A committee will spend as much time
> as necessary to perpetuate itself, ex-
> clusive of its reason for existence.

These homegrown homilies, all encountered during
my research on Murphy's Law, are pure Parkinson,
but they are also mild Murphy. Old Murph tends
to put the worst possible complexion on things.
He would probably have gone overboard and said
something like:

> Large blocks of time set aside to ac-
> complish trivial tasks will be ex-
> ceeded.

Parkinson merely theorizes a dead heat. Nevertheless he has stumbled onto something of fairly
cosmic proportions, something that transcends the
time-work relationship with which he was dealing.
What we're really looking at here is nature's abhor-
rence of a vacuum. The Parkinsonian proverb can
thus be stated in the abstract as :

$$A \text{ expands to fill } B$$

where "A" is variable and "B" is fixed. One need
only select parameters willy-nilly and all the hectic
squeeze plays of life can be illustrated. I give you
more real-life contributions:

> A bathroom hook will be loaded to
> capacity immediately upon becoming
> available.

> Expenditures expand to meet the
> available budget.

The occupation of space expands to
usurp all that is available, regardless
of need.

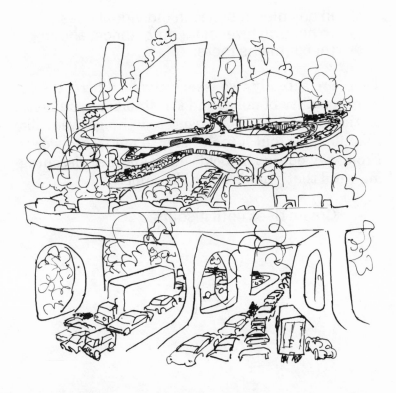

A freeway is glutted beyond capacity
the day it opens.

I could go on but I seem to have already (A) filled
the available page (B).

Peter's Law

This popular polemic on the corporate pecking order
is not to be scoffed at simply because it sounds
reasonable. And it does sound reasonable:

> In any hierarchy, each individual rises
> to his own level of incompetence, and
> then remains there.

There are actually two issues involved here: the up-
ward mobility of dolts, and the stabilizing influence
of their bungling. We suspected things were like
that all along, but it took Peter to put it into words.
From way out in left field comes another discourag-
ing word that sounds much the same:

> Cream rises until it sours.

However, here is a disquieting variation gleaned from a house organ in Flushing, New York:

> If many individuals remain too long at their level of incompetence, they will destroy the organization because their presence demonstrates to others that competence is not a prerequisite for success.

This looks good on the surface but it suffers from an excess of logic. Actually, it is pure nonsense. It is

clearly understood by all participants in the Hierarchy Game that competence is no prerequisite for
success. Buoyancy is. That, and a facility for keeping one's chin up when the tide comes in.

If Peter's Law sounds like carping from the
hierarchical underbrush, the whole concept can be
overturned and viewed from the top down:

> The longevity of an employee is in-
> versely proportional to the quality of
> his work. The more inept he is, the
> harder it is to get rid of him.

Many executives swear this is the real law, but alas,
it turns out to be nothing more than the original
proposition in disguise. Just because incompetents
prosper on the bottom rungs, this in no way reveals
ability at the top. Some people merely reach their
level of incompetence quicker than others. In fact,
some of us are born there.

The question then remains: If it is Peter, is it
also Murphy? Probably not. Murphy's Law deals
with man's inability to deal effectively with intelligent, remorseless, inanimate objects. On the
other hand, Peter's axiom pits people against one
another, and incompetent people at that. Once
again the lesser law comes off as weak tea to Murphy's Mickey Finn.

And, finally, a brief potpourri of minor in-
dignities:

Sergeant Preston's Posterior Prognosis

The average individual's position in the hierarchy is a lot like pulling a dogsled—there's no change of scenery except for the lead dog.

This law is a great consolation for people who like to face the issue head on.

The Sunsweet Law of Perpetual Movement

Never eat prunes when you are famished.

Violation of this law is said to cure a cough by default.

Dr. Doolittle's Alimentary Deduction

Never, never play leapfrog with a unicorn.

If this law fails to make an impression on you, you have missed the point.

Russell's Decree of Disproportionate Dispersal

Whatever strikes a fan is not evenly distributed.

This is also known as the How-Come-It-All-Landed-On-Me Law. It comes as close to the quintessence of Murphy's Law as anything you'll find in Pie Theory. It is simple and direct. It is universal in application. It deals with your classic inanimate object, and it is perversity incarnate. Armed with this law alone, one may look back on a lifetime of futile endeavor and say, "Truly, my fan runneth over."

As we go to press, several new and highly entertaining laws have come to my attention, among them:

Wha....

[Editor's note: The remainder of Mr. Russell's manuscript is spattered with a dense substance to the extent that we can't make it out. Oh, well.]

My life is a tribute to the efficacy of Murphy's Law. I entered the Army with a chemist's rating, was sent to training schools in the Field Artillery and Medical Corps, then spent the Korean conflict as a supply sergeant in the Corps of Engineers. Graduating from college, my only aim was to steer clear of the accounting profession—a profession for which I had neither interest nor ability. Naturally, my first job was as an accountant.

My other major career aversion (I have no penchants, only aversions) was to stay out of my father's footsteps—writing. For the past nineteen years I have been employed as a full time writer.

Jim Russell